DEVON LIBRARIES	
D12117014X0100	
Bertrams	30/09/2010
385.361	£14.95
TP	

'EXETER MEMORIES'
EXMOUTH JUNCTION FIREMAN

Richard Parkinson

© Noodle Books and Richard Parkinson 2010

ISBN 978-1-906419-40-0

First published in 2010 by Kevin Robertson under the **NOODLE BOOKS** imprint
PO Box 279, Corhampton, SOUTHAMPTON. SO32 3ZX

The Publisher and Author hereby give notice that all rights to this work are reserved. Aside from brief passages for the purpose of review, no part of this work may be reproduced, copied by electronic or other means, or otherwise stored in any information storage and retrieval system without written permission from the Publisher. This includes the illustrations herein which shall remain the copyright of the copyright holder unless otherwise stated.

www.noodlebooks.co.uk

Printed in England by Ian Allan Printing Ltd.

Note - All unaccredited views were taken by the Author or from his own collection.

Front cover - AWS fitted Merchant Navy, No. 35025 'Brocklebank Line' on the disposal road at Exmouth Junction.

Frontispiece - One of our 'Woolworths'. 'N', No. 31853 in typical 'Meldon Brown' livery. The engine is complete with an '83D', ex-Laira, then Exmouth Junction diesel alloy shedplate.

Rear cover - All my own work on an '800' tank'!

Dedicated to my late parents, Syd and Marjorie - who fostered my interest in all things steam.

I would also add grateful thanks to my daughters: Elaine, Lindsey, Bryony and Elisabeth, who kept telling me to "Get on and do it". Well now I have - and I hope you like it!

Richard Parkinson, Exeter, 2010

CONTENTS

EXMOUTH JUNCTION - AN INTRODUCTION TO STEAM	5
RECOLLECTIONS IN COLOUR	9
MONOCHROME MEMORIES	17
TRAVELS IN COLOUR - OKEHAMPTON, ST JAMES PARK HALT, EXETER CENTRAL	25
A FIREMAN ON THE MAIN LINE	33
THE INTERLOPER AT ST. DAVID'S	41
A JOB FOR LIFE?	51
'BLUE PETER'	55
MEMORIES	56

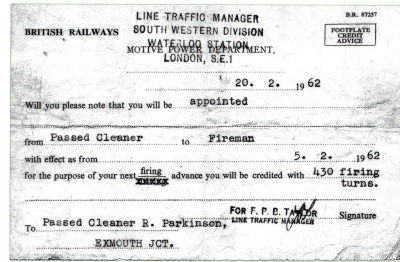

An '800', or to be more accurate, a BR 'Standard Class 4'. This is No. 80035, seen at St. David's with ballast hoppers. Driver Morris Beavan is leaning from the cab window. This was first of the '800' type we had at Exmouth Junction and they were grand engines. No. 80035 was also the locomotive involved in the incident with 'Gold Braid', at Budleigh Salterton, described on page 6.

EXMOUTH JUNCTION - AN INTRODUCTION TO STEAM

When I left school in 1959, aged 15 it was with the ambition to forge a career in commercial art. Yes, I had always been keen on railways, steam especially, and had for some time previous been a member of the 'Platform 5 Group' at Exeter St David's. Additionally I was in what was then the obligatory organisation for loco-spotters, the Ian Allan Locospotters Club; I still have the different colour Western and Southern Regions badges. Consequently after leaving school, it was straight to Exeter College of Art, where for a couple of terms I was compelled to, "...paint what you feel, not what you see…", hardly the introduction to my ambition.

Father was a traditional sign writer of considerable local standing, who fortunately also knew everyone, so upon expressing my disappointment about the college course, I asked if he might know how I could instead join the railway, with obvious ambitions of becoming a driver. Here it was then that Father's contacts were useful, for upon the advice of a friend of his, he took me to St David's both of us full of enthusiasm, only to be told that at 15 I was too young for footplate training, you had to be 17, and although they would take me on, for the first two years it would be as a wagon axle-box oiler at Exeter Riverside yard.

Luckily Dad had another mate. This one already worked at Exeter Central, and through him an appointment was made with Mr Horace Moore, Shedmaster at Exmouth Junction. Here the reception was different. My age of 15 was fine, and "...subject to passing a medical I had a job for life". With hindsight such a statement might appear strange, but it was said with genuine belief, after all the railways had continued in much the same way for generations, and no one could have foreseen the changes that would happen just a few short years into the future.

Having convinced the doctors that everything was in the right place and operating correctly, I arrived for the start of my new career. The Southern Region were short of footplate crews at that time and promotion was rumoured to be fairly swift. Even so, for the first few weeks, my job was as one of the Messengers, carrying mails from the depot to the 'Control' Locomotive Office, located at Exeter Central station. This involved lots of travel from Polsloe Bridge Halt on the Exmouth Branch, the nearest official stopping place to the shed. Sometimes it was possible to cadge a lift on an engine leaving or retuning to the depot, which to me was a far better option. Thus was my introduction to the railway, at the time always working an 8am to 4pm shift.

Evidently the shortages I had heard of were true, for after just a few weeks I was transferred to cleaning, this time on either 6am to 2pm or 2pm to 10pm shift. There was also a night cleaning shift, but I was exempt from night work due to being just 15 at the time. In addition to cleaning we had to do any odd jobs, one in particular I recall as being very unpopular, the carrying of 1 cwt bags of cotton waste - used for cleaning, on our backs across several shed roads. Another was 'oiling the underneath', to save some of the older main line drivers the task. One driver I remember, used to give us 2/6d to chuck the whole contents of a gallon can of cylinder oil over the inside big ends of his rebuilt 'Merchant Navy' prior to going to Salisbury.

Naturally jobs such as these were giving us an insight into the workings of the locomotive itself. The months passed quickly, especially as I already knew some of the other young cleaners who had been at the same school as me. The time then came for a group of us to be sent to the Exeter Central Firing School, a grand name for a none too grand grounded coach body close to the loco office.

Here we were taught the mechanics of firing by Inspector Edgar Snow, together with an introduction to the Rule Book with great emphasis on the all important 'Rule 55'. (Train protection when stationary.) We also learnt single line token and tablet working, demonstrations on the exchange of the latter involving a brass tablet inscribed, 'Chelfham - Blackmoor', taken from the long closed Lynton and Barnstaple line. After this, a quick exam with Mr Moore followed: questions on the Rule Book and then outside to name the various parts of the Walschaerts valve gear on a 'Z' class 0-8-0T, conveniently parked nearby on No. 1 road. I must have satisfied the powers that be, for henceforth I became officially a 'Passed Cleaner' and so eligible for firing turns.

The first of these came shortly afterwards, on Christmas Eve 1960. The engine was a 'Z' class, No. 30956 'on the bank', as we referred to the steep climb from Exeter St David's up to Exeter Central. Looking back, these engines were just great on this job, plenty of power and plenty of grip. They had replaced the smaller 'E1R' type, although I never had the chance to work on one of these smaller 0-6-2T types.

Various turns followed, Loco Shunting, more Banking, and Exmouth Junction yard shunting - a lot of the latter. Often this was on members of the 'Z' type, but also on 'M7's and 'Ivatt' Class 2 engines. I recall one driver on 'The Yard', whose name I had better not mention even nearly 50 years later. He, being satisfied that his young fireman could drive the engine, would retire to the locomen's club on the other side of the main line not to be seen again for some time. Totally against all the rules, there was now just one man on the footplate. So far as the actual work was concerned, this was fine if we had a 'Z' fitted with a steam reverser, but if, as we did later on, have a former GWR 'Pannier Tank' with 'strong-arm' lever reverse, or an 'Ivatt' with screw reverse, it was a different story. Under such circumstances and with such duties, it was noticeable how some drivers: those that did not leave the footplate that is, and who were otherwise reluctant to relinquish their side of the footplate to a junior fireman to gain experience, seemed to change their minds.

Later, and after amassing the required number of firing turns, I was made up to a Fireman proper. Again there was a test, but mine was a doddle, a 'topped and tailed' ballast train, meaning a train with an engine at the front and another shoving at the rear, from Exeter, the 17 or so miles to Honiton. I was on the 'S15' at the front: there was an 'N' at the back end, and watching over my every move was Inspector Charlie Roke. I don't remember a lot about the trip, expect there was a lot of standing about between bouts of shunting and me having to make frequent trips to make the tea. Charlie told me I made a good 'cuppa', he did not say a lot about my firing, except that is when we reached Honiton when he informed me I had passed, then he presumably went home 'pass', (- meaning 'on the cushions' in a passenger train), as we never saw him again on that duty.

I was put into the 'Exmouth' gang, which, as the name implies, covered the branch line of that name. However, it was not just on trains from Exeter to Exmouth, as there was the Sidmouth branch which also reached Exmouth this time via Tipton St Johns. At this time, Exmouth Junction had just started to receive its first batch of 'Standard' Class 4 tanks engines in the 80xxx series. Initially these were on loan from other depots: presumably to see if they were suitable, a formal allocation came later. Because of their numbers, we referred to them as the '800' tanks. The turns were shared with the smaller 'Ivatt' Class 2 engines. Initially I was with Driver 'Taff' Burridge, being told by another young fireman that he was a bit of a miserable old so and so. That warning certainly seemed to be the case, that is until one day when we were taking our break at Sidmouth Junction. I got out my small transistor radio (- remember that is what we called them…?),
intending to take my grub and sit on the grass bank alongside the engine. On seeing me with the radio, 'Taff' commented, "Here Ray", - he always called me Ray (never did know why), "Can you get the racing on that thing?". I responded that I guessed so, and turned the dial accordingly. Having found the station, he listened intently. Fortunately his bets that day must have been successful, as afterwards he always asked me to, "Bring the wireless". In return I was allowed to drive on occasions. Other firemen would enquire what I had done to get on with him so well, but I never let them into the secret.

I mentioned that this was the time we were getting the '800' tanks, and Taff and I had No. 80035 from Sidmouth Junction to Exmouth. It happened this was the first time one of the class had used the route, whereupon arrival at Budleigh Salterton, 'Taff' was immediately confronted by the resident Station Master - gold braid and all, "Driver, what do you mean by bringing that large engine into MY station", the emphasis being that it was definitely he who was in charge. 'Taff' responded simply, "I just drive what I'm given", at which point the Guard blew his whistle and we departed, Taff with his usual blasting departure. These locos really revolutionised workings on many of our jobs and were the true masters of everything thrown at them.

Before leaving the 'Exmouth', one amusing incident comes to mind. Again it was with 'Taff' and with another '800', this time bunker first coming up the bank and under the A30 roadway towards Sidmouth Junction. Immediately after this bridge, the cutting dropped away to be replaced on one side by several railway houses whose gardens led down to the trackside. One of the occupants of these houses, I recall now probably a signalman, had asked Taff beforehand to 'drop off a bit of coal' into his garden as we passed. Ever happy to oblige, Taff had agreed, whereupon I was instructed accordingly and had made ready a very large single piece, weighing we estimated well over 1 cwt. It should keep him happy for some time. So, as we approached the designated spot, I manoeuvred said lump into position by the cab door. Taff was still blasting away, plenty of regulator, (- he always did drive that way), when, as instructed I put my boot against the lump and shoved. Whether it was our speed, a rough piece of track at that point, or just bad luck, I don't know. What I do know is that as the lump landed it bounced - shades of the Barnes Wallace bouncing bomb perhaps, straight through the wooden garden fence and continued in like fashion towards his greenhouse. We watched as the whole event unfolded, seemingly in slow motion, as next came the signalman's greenhouse, which it proceeded to enter, unfortunately via the end WITHOUT the door. I never heard further, but have wondered to this day whether it even 'exploded' as it eventually came to rest. Happy days…… .

After the Exmouth, I did a stint as a 'Merchant Navy' fireman. In case the reader might think I had been identified as so good at my job that I

With the concrete monolith which served as the coal stage prominent, the dirt and debris associated with any steam shed, certainly not just Exmouth Junction, is apparent. On the right is No. 34015, 'Exmouth', whilst on the left is a glimpse of the crane that was used to clear clinker from the disposal pits.

was considered suitable for main line work that quickly, think again. This was simple preparation and disposal work, signing on, I think, at 8.00 am., and preparing the engines that would work the 10.30 am. and 12.30 pm. trains to Waterloo. Together with my driver, we also had the job of disposing of the engines off the 9.00 am. and 11.00 am. ex Waterloo services. After this came the 'Junior Spare Link', and where the fun really began, as, apart generally from true main line work, we could get literally any train going.

My first driver in this link was George Leverton, a great man, but who sadly died young. Despite being officially paired with George, I also spent much time with different men, on loan to Yeovil (a lot) Bude, or Barnstaple Junction (not much). I also covered work from the sheds at Okehampton, Lyme Regis and Seaton, all of which were sub-depots to Exmouth Junction.

I recall once arriving at Yeovil and upon reporting to the Foreman being told, "You'll be on the Weymouth banker, it's a Pannier Tank….", and he gave me the number. I found the engine but straight away it did not look very lively. I had a closer look and the reason was obvious: the fire had been allowed to go out. Reporting back, we were instead given a member of the 'U' class. Unfortunately all this had taken valuable time, allied to which the engine was facing tender first towards Weymouth. Ideal for our run down, but less than ideal for our banking duties. We ended up banking two trains tender-first on Evershot bank. Another 'on-loan' turn found me at Barnstaple with no one present at the shed. I tried but there was just no one around, so spent the whole day there without seeing a soul and returned at the due time having achieved nothing but a sun tan.

From Exmouth Junction, we would also cover the Seaton branch when required. Here there were 'M7' 0-4-4Ts, fitted for pull-push working with Westinghouse air pumps. Because 'pull-push' meant we would be legitimately alone on the footplate for every other trip. Several of us went 'passenger' to Seaton with Inspector Sam Smith, feared by us all, but who was evidently sufficiently impressed to pass each one of us. After this one of us would cover for the regular Seaton fireman whenever necessary. If this was for a late turn, we were supposed to lodge in an old coach at Seaton, but nearly everyone took their bike and cycled to Axminster to catch a down working which stopped at Axminster but not at Seaton Junction. Later, when the M7s were retired, we were given GWR 'Pannier Tanks' and Auto-Coaches, again push-pull operation but controlled by mechanical instead of air operation and which involved connecting a heavy and unwieldy sliding steel coupling so the driver might control the regulator from the front. I seem to recall Nos. 6412 and 6430 were two of the engines involved at this time. Because of the difficulty with this bar coupling the regulator, we adopted the practice of running with this uncoupled, and meaning I controlled the regulator myself whilst the driver, in the front portion of the coach had the brake. This worked fine - provided the fireman maintained his concentration on where he was and was not distracted by the need to attend to the fire or other issues. I recall once we had a smaller WR type, an 0-4-2T No. 1450, (- we also had No. 1442 at times), running into Colyford when I took my eye off the ball and we stopped with a heck of a jerk as the driver applied full braking with me still having the regulator full open. You can imagine what was said, but I was not the first and would not be the last either. I recall the names of the regular Seaton branch drivers as Dan Weston and Harold Pope.

Around this time, 1963, I had been on the railway some four years and was shortly to have, what was up to that time, would be my greatest railway experience. I was asked by another Exmouth Junction man, Fireman Smith, if I would swap a duty with him so he could attend a wedding. Said Fireman was a main line man, paired to one of the Top Link drivers, Les Billings. The turn started on the 3.20 pm. Exeter to Templecombe with an 'S15' and return with a down goods behind a rebuilt 'Light Pacific'. Les was known as a fast driver, but before I could go with him and because I was still junior, the duty swap had to be authorised by Mr. Moore the Shedmaster. To our mutual relief, the swap was authorised and I duly signed on. The engine had already been prepared, some other poor soul had that task, so we backed down to Central and hooked on.

Les lived up to his reputation from the start, and he literally thrashed 'the black un' - as we called the 'S15's, all the way, whistle screaming as we passed through Blackboy Tunnel. Initially I was just hanging on, but as we passed Exmouth Junction he turned to me and said, 'Get firing Son'. I just piled it in, no finesse, if it went thought the door fine, if not I would try and sweep it up later. We tore past Exmouth Junction shed, where a group of cleaners who had come out to cheer us on. It was an enjoyable and certainly swift run, but one which was over far too soon. Sadly too the only chance I ever had to work with Les.

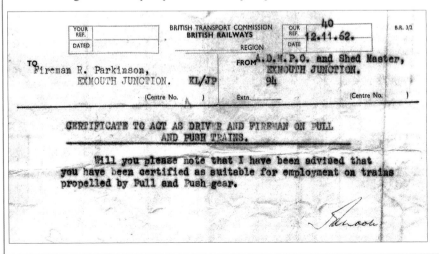

RECOLLECTIONS IN COLOUR

No. 35006, 'Peninsular and Oriental S. N. Co' at Exmouth Junction. It was on this engine that I had my fastest trip on the main line: 98½ mph through Broadclyst with Driver Alfie Cook - see page 33.

Above - No. 34079 '141 Squadron' - a good tidy engine. **Right** - In reasonably clean condition - at least the green livery can be discerned, is No. 34015 'Exmouth'. Apart from one month in 1950, this engine was allocated to Exmouth Junction from August 1950 through to August 1964 when it was transferred to Salisbury. Just visible amidst the supporting metal braces of the water tower, is the signal arm used for testing the eye sight of drivers: who were expected to be able to tell the indication from the other end of the yard. (Indicated by the arrow on the illustration.) I once stopped for a 'blow-up' (- meaning shortage of steam), with 34015 at Honiton Tunnel on a down train. The cause was not me, but a firebox full of clinker.

No. 34107 'Blandford Forum' with discs up ready to run light engine to Exeter Central. Alongside, is No. 34003 'Plymouth'.

'Around the depot.' **Left** - Another 'Woolworth', so nicknamed as they were allegedly built on the cheap at the former Woolwich Arsenal, inside the 'Lifting Road'. It was here that all major repairs were carried out under the eye of Foreman Fitter, Charlie Smaile. The engine is 'N' No. 31845, another long term depot resident. **Top** - The interior gloom of the shed. **Bottom** - The old steam crane, of antiquarian vintage, used for clearing clinker and ash from the disposal pit and lifting it into wagons. There was a regular driver for this machine, in my time it was Fred Messenger. It was later replaced by a more modern, Smith-Rodley, machine.

Left - Disposal of a rebuilt 'Merchant Navy' - in this case No. 35006. The 'M.N.' duty Fireman is shovelling the accumulation of ash from the smokebox, his eyes already squinting from the particles that blow around. On the ground Driver Bill Godbeer will place his hand on the various joints to check nothing has been running 'hot'. *Above* - 'Ivatt Class 2' No. 41295, one of the type with screw reverse that made them less than ideal for shunting, but they were great little engines on the branch lines.

MONOCHROME MEMORIES

Left - No. 34059, 'Sir Archibald Sinclair' a Salisbury based engine but recorded by me at Exmouth Junction. Following withdrawal from Salisbury in 1966, it rusticated away until being reborn on the Bluebell Railway in the summer of 2009. Like most men at my depot, we loved these rebuilt engines.

Top - No. 34006 'Bude' on the turntable with Driver Jack Craggs in the cab - I was working the turntable. The engine had arrived 'light' after a privately sponsored tour from Waterloo to Sidmouth Junction. It was being made ready for the return light to Sidmouth Junction and then with the train again to Waterloo. April 1966.
S J Healey

Right - The same engine, this time being coaled. The small concrete hut lower left, was the coalman's cabin.

S J Healey

Top left - *Following the withdrawal of the various pre-group Southern types, we began to see more and more of the 'Standard' designs - the '800' series tank engines have of course already been mentioned - one (No. 80064) is seen behind the tender version of this 'Class 4', No. 75025. Behind both was one of the former WR engines we saw on-shed towards the latter days of steam, 0-6-0 No. 3205, which served duty as one of our last snowplough fitted engines.*

Top right - *Somewhat travel weary 'West Country' No. 34002 'Salisbury' out of steam and waiting to go on to the lifting road - the other side of the crane. (The latter was the machine that was steamed when required. Its sole purpose was to lift off, and then back on, the streamlined casings of the original Bulleid engines: I never saw it move from this position.)*

Top - 'Z' No. 30951 cautiously enters Platform 3 at St David's ready to buffer up and bank a train to Exeter Central, 20 August 1959. I had my first firing turn on sister engine No. 30956 on Christmas Eve 1960 on the same duty. The class were superb for this work, incredibly strong although due to their short wheelbase they did tend to lurch about a bit. The steep gradient between the two Exeter stations meant that even an engine as strong as a 'Z' was limited to just a 200 ton load on the 1 in 37 bank. The same engine is seen again at the end of its days and awaiting a call to the scrap yard on page 23.

Tony Molyneaux

Bottom - Another interloper, 'Pannier tank' No 3759 alongside No. 34014 'Budleigh Salterton'. Following the demise of 'Z' class and also their replacement SR 'W' type tanks, we had BR 'Standard' tank engines and also these 'Pannier Tanks' for use on banking trains up from St. David's. Despite being a Southern man I will have to admit they were a very strong little engine. (Even allowing for my liking for these engines, I have to admit their capability on banking duty was somewhat less than the engines they had replaced.)

Opposite bottom left - Another engine to survive into preservation was No. 34007 'Wadebridge' recorded here on the disposal pit. To the left is the metalwork of the water tank supports, at the base of which the little brick shed is where the chemist worked analysing the water supply. According to his instructions, we would drop the required number of briquettes into the tender to soften the water and so reduce impurities and the formation of scale. The latter especially would otherwise coat the tubes inside the boiler, so reducing the amount of heat that might otherwise pass through and thus restrict steam generation. This was known 'T.I.A.' water treatment. Another advantage of such treated water, was that the time span between necessary boiler wash-outs could be markedly increased. The briquettes themselves would arrive at the depots in yellow barrels. One unfortunately side effect of the treated water was that it tended to have a detrimental effect on the paintwork of the engines.

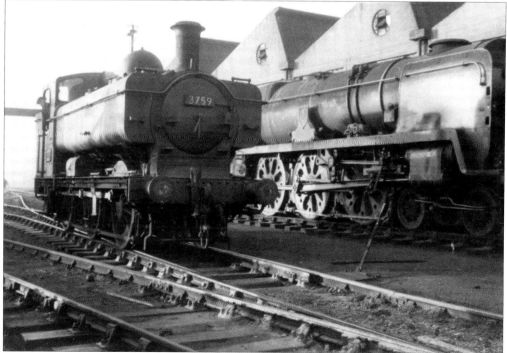

Far left - *Fireman Richard Parkinson in the cab of No. 34006 'Bude' in 1964.* S J Healey

Left - *Head on view of No. 34021 'Dartmoor' alongside the breakdown train at Exmouth Junction. The view was taken off the back of the tender of a WR '2251' class acting as our snowplough engine - possibly No. 3205.*

Above - *A pair of AWS fitted 'Woolworths' (- does that then mean a 'Special Offer?), Nos. 31835 and 31841 at Exmouth Junction with 'Z' No. 30955 identifiable in the background. At some stage there has evidently been a shortage of headcode discs, as witness the chalk mark at the top of the smokebox on No. 31841.*

Tony Molyneaux

Far left - Driver 'Taff' Burridge and myself on No. 80035 at Sidmouth Junction in December 1962.   *The late A Thomas*

Left and above - The end of the road for one of our 'Z' class engines together with a number of other Southern stalwarts. The scene is Exeter St David's loco shed, with the engines, Nos. 30951, 30700, 31409, 30697 and 30689. The last two listed, both members of the '700' class, had previously been used as our 'snowplough' engines, see page 33, and were replaced by a WR '2251' type, as seen earlier. Previously they had been stripped of any re-usable parts before being sent for scrap.

This page - The mundane but essential work at Meldon Quarry. The furthest west a 'USA' ever reached, DS234, formerly No. 30062, worked here from 1962 until 1966. In 1966, I had expressed an interest in perhaps buying this very engine when it came out of service and was indeed offered it for £400 in what was reasonable working order. Unfortunately I could not raise the required sum in time.

Opposite - High summer at Okehampton shed. We had just arrived with No. 34033 'Chard' on the Surbiton - Okehampton car-carrier train which we had worked from Exeter. After turning the engine ready for the return to Exeter, I had taken a break from shovelling coal forward to take the photograph - hence the shovel seen sticking out of the top of the tender. On another occasion I was disposing of this same engine which had arrived with an awful lot of fire still in the firebox. On starting to drop this, it set light to the inside of the casing: where oil thrown up from the motion would soak into the lagging. The old dodge, known to all, was to quickly move the engine alongside a water column and put the bag through the cab window and so into the gap alongside the casing: an inrush of water would then flood the fire out. It worked, but not before No. 34033 had lived up to its name, although now spelt slightly differently, 'Charred'.

TRAVELS IN COLOUR - OKEHAMPTON, ST JAMES PARK HALT, EXETER CENTRAL

ST JAMES PARK HALT

Light Engines at St James Park Halt.

Opposite - No. 34107 'Blandford Forum' has left its train at Exeter Central and is running back towards the depot at Exmouth Junction. The engine is just about to pass under Lions Holt Bridge, officially Bridge No. 527, the stopping place was also called 'Lions Holt Halt' until 1946 when a name change took place to reflect its proximity to the Exeter City football ground of St James Park.

This page, top left - No. 34039 'Boscastle' on a similar return trip, complete with headcode discs for the main line and a tail lamp.

This page, top right - Without any indication as to its destination, but probably again the depot, Standard 'Class 3' No. 82039 runs through the platforms.

This page, bottom right - Having come off a North Devon line working, 'N' No. 31843 runs towards Exmouth Junction.

ST JAMES PARK HALT

Above - *Empties for Meldon, behind No. 34108 'Wincanton'.*
Opposite page, top left - *No. 34095 'Brentor' running back towards Exeter Central ready to take up a Salisbury / Waterloo working.*
Opposite page, top right - *'800' type, (BR Standard 'Class 4') No. 80037 on LMR stock, possibly a through / excursion working. Few main line services called at St. James Park Halt and instead it was served by certain of the Exmouth branch trains.*
Opposite page, bottom left - *An unidentified 'West Country' near journeys end at Exeter Central.*
Opposite page, bottom right - *One of the larger 'Merchant Navy' class engines, No. 35013 'Blue Funnel' passing through. The engine will be detached at Exeter Central as the type were not permitted to run on the Southern lines west of Exeter.*

ST JAMES PARK HALT

This page and opposite top left - No. 35008 'Orient Line' backing down onto an eastbound service and preparing for departure.
Opposite, top right - A somewhat travel stained No. 34032 'Camelford' released from its train and with the tail lamp affixed and disc signal cleared is setting off to return to Exmouth Junction.
Opposite, bottom left - No. 34056 'Croydon' in the process of making up its train, (- the addition of the restaurant car portion at Exeter Central on to the coaches already arrived from west of Exeter involved a degree of shunting).
Opposite, bottom right - Journey's end for No. 35026 'Lamport & Holt Line' arriving Platform 2 at Exeter Central.

EXETER CENTRAL

LINES TO EXMOUTH

Top left - *M7s at Exmouth 2 September 1962. No. 30025 is in the process of running round - No. 30024 will undertake the same manoeuvre shortly, after which the then empty train will be drawn back to be stabled away from the platform until the time comes to shunt back in ready for departure. Andrew Westlake collection.*
Top right and bottom right - *Exmouth Terminus seen from the station throat. The multitude of signals allowed all four platform faces to be used for departures either to Exeter or Sidmouth Junction.* ***Bottom left*** - *From the south end of the platform at Tipton St. Johns, is seen the divergence of the Sidmouth branch: left, and Budleigh Salterton / Exmouth route to the right. Peter Elliott - 3.*

A FIREMAN ON THE MAIN LINE

Having perhaps proved my worth, I had a week on the main line soon afterwards. The high spot of which was with 'Merchant Navy' No. 35006 with only nine coaches on the down 1 o'clock. We had taken over the train at Salisbury, already with an almost full firebox, meaning I had little to do save pulling it through. I recall I did not touch the fire after Templecombe, so to try and reduce some of the excess, my driver, Alfie Cook, stated, "Let's see if we can get the ton". We tore through Broadclyst with the regulator in the roof and the speedo reading 98½ mph! A memorable occasion. Despite his efforts, it did not work, we arrived at Exeter with the engine still making steam and blowing off. The fire dropper was not going to be pleased when the engine reached the shed!

Then it was back to the mundane, the odd special to Okehampton, such as with No 34033 'Chard' on page 25 although before all of this, a most interesting little trip.

I have already described my first firing turn 'on the bank', so it may now be appropriate to describe in detail what was in fact my very first actual main-line firing turn. Perhaps surprisingly this was on a passenger working and a special to boot: possibly with hindsight the very fact it was an extra working meant I was probably fortunate enough to be selected.

The train was from Sidmouth Junction to Exeter Central via Exmouth, double headed with two M7s Nos. 30024 and 30025. (The actual service was an enthusiasts working of 2 September 1962, originating and then returning to Waterloo from Exeter but via Eastleigh on the return journey.) Both the engines had been especially cleaned - even the headboard discs had been freshly painted Consequently this was a full main line train and occupied the whole platform at Exmouth. Here also the party would have a break, so after the coaches had emptied we placed the stock in the 'Docks' siding within the goods yard. Both crews then banked down the fires on the engines and I expected to be able to put my feet up for a while before continuing. But Ted Bainborough my driver had other ideas and called, 'Come on, let's go through the train".

At the time I was not aware of what he might have in mind, but as he was the driver, I followed his lead. We climbed up into the first coach and I quickly saw Ted putting his hand down the back of the seats. Here he would find various coins: I was quick to follow his example. After checking through the whole train in the manner, we had enough for a couple of pints at the nearby Railwaymen's Club. Clearly I still had a lot to learn.

When departure time came we had both engines ready and literally thrashed our way back to Exeter Central, non-stop, running bunker first. A good day out as well. I learnt later that Ted must clearly have displayed initiative in other areas, for he subsequently became Loco Inspector Ted Bainborough.

Like many, I recall the severe winter of 1963, cold, snow and then as the thaw set in, floods. In the snow period - which lasted without respite form the end of December through to March, I recall being booked on a late spare turn with driver Ken Davey. As a 'spare' crew, we were at the mercy of both the shed foreman and control and so might be called upon to cover for a crew who had not arrived or were late: this could happen if a booked working was itself running late, or for any untoward or emergency situation that might arise. This time it was the latter, as the running foreman rushed into the 'cabin' where we were ourselves nicely warm - hoping perhaps we might not to have to venture out during that shift.

The news was not good, " ...an up goods was buried on Sourton Moor on the edge of Dartmoor between Okehampton and Lydford." It was time for 'The Ploughs'.

At this time Exmouth Junction maintained two '700' class 0-6-0 engines, or 'Blackmotors' as the type were referred to, and just for this duty. Consequently the heavy snowploughs were already attached. The engines, at this time, Nos. 30697 and 30689, were also kept in steam almost continuously so as to be ready at a moment's notice.

The two plough engines were coupled tender to tender and besides the crew, a fitter and loco inspector were on board. Leading, and facing towards Okehampton on No. 30697 were Driver Stan Milton and Fireman Joe Baker accompanied by Fitter Johnny Watts. My driver on No. 30689 was Ken Davey and Inspector Charlie Roke was riding with us. My memory may be failing at this point, as I seem to recall there may even have been another fitter riding with us as well.

Whatever, by the time we set off it was completely dark although there was not much snow at Exeter, indeed we hardly seemed to encounter much at all until we neared Okehampton. Beyond Okehampton and over Meldon we entered the cutting leading to Meldon Junction signal box and it was as we exited the cutting here that the situation suddenly changed. The wind chill became intense, so intense in fact the injectors on the engine froze almost at once and consequently blew-out - meaning no water was reaching the injector from the tender, it also meant it was so cold the whole thing had iced up whilst it had still been working. This was despite the fact they were both in operation and consequently much hotter than the ambient temperature.

When we did find the stopped goods, the engine of which was a 'Woolworth', the crew from it had already thrown the fire out, not expecting to get any further. We found out later they had also taken refuge in a nearby pub - presumably also from where they had raised the alarm, although the signalmen on either side would probably already have been alerted to the fact something was wrong as the train had been an unusually long time in section.

Not surprisingly the goods had also stuck on what was one of the most exposed sections of line, right as mentioned earlier, on the edge of Dartmoor itself and where the wind had blown the snow into deep drifts.

As we attempted to plough our way through these drifts to get closer to the trapped engine, we ourselves stuck. We tried to reverse out but that was no good either. Charlie Roke then made the decision to uncouple our two engines, the idea being that if it was the lead engine that was itself stuck, we might have a chance of reversing back out. Fortunately the couplings had not iced up, but as we reversed back so the tender of our own engine became derailed on impacted snow. Such was the ferocity of the weather that this snow had accumulated in a short space of time.

A quick conference with the crew on the lead engine revealed they too had lost their injectors. There was nothing now we could do and it was agreed that to remain in what were such exposed conditions was actually life threatening to us all. It was time to throw the fires out and seek safety elsewhere. By now also much time had elapsed and again concerned that nothing had been heard I learned later that a further rescue train had been sent out from the direction of Okehampton. From a distance we later saw the headlights of the engine from this rescue train, but conditions were deteriorating all the time and they could not reach us. (I learned later it was No. 34108 'Wincanton' with the Exmouth Junction breakdown train.)

Gathering up our few belongings we set off as a group for Sourton village, passing in the process through the churchyard. Here the snow was so deep we would sink down to our knees and then trip over the tops of the gravestones. We made it to the 'Highwayman' pub, certainly prepared to stay the night. Charlie Roke though was conscious of the situation and the need to try and reopen the line as soon as possible. He thus arranged for help in the form of a D63xx diesel with the breakdown train from Laira to arrive from the opposite direction. It was by this means that we finally travelled back to Plymouth North Road and got a lift back to Exeter St David's in the guard's van of a night goods via the WR coastal route with the seas breaking over us at Dawlish. Our own two engines and that of the goods would remain stuck for a while longer.

Another time, still during the same winter, I was on the 4.00 pm late spare, (I did see daylight sometimes), and had managed to cadge a lift to the depot from Exeter Central on a light engine. As we were passing the pointsman's hut at the entrance to the depot I saw my driver for the shift, Ralphie Bartlett, passing me and leaving the depot on foot. He must have been expecting me to arrive in this fashion - as I often did, and so looked up to the engine. On seeing me he yelled out, "I'm just off for more grub, we're in for a long night." Unfortunately I was not in a position to copy his example so it was certainly not the sort of news I was pleased to hear at that time.

I signed on and reported to the running foreman. Here I was told to prepare a rebuilt 'Bulleid', from memory I think it was No. 34062 '17 Squadron'. The foreman had not imparted anything else at this stage, perhaps working on the basis that the news had already been given to the driver and as a mere fireman I was too lowly to bother wasting more breath upon.

Whatever, I arrived at No. 34062 and set about 'waking it up' as we called it. Ralphie arrived shortly afterwards and said, "We've got to pick up our train from the yard....". He now told me we were collecting a rake of empty ballast wagons, 'Mermaids' was their official designation, together with two brake vans. These would be used as travelling

This page - *The morning after the night before. '700's Nos, 30689: left, and 30697, ice bound and marooned after our abortive attempts to reach the stranded train.*

Western Morning News

Left - *A mere sprinkling at Exeter Central in 1963. the enclosed cab of No. 80064 was the ideal place to be.*

The late W S G Parkinson

accommodation for a group of hardy souls from the p/way department who we were to transport and hopefully dig out a passenger train trapped in snow between Sampford Courtney and Okehampton.

Having collected the wagons, we stopped in the middle road at Exeter Central to allow the men to board. As we did this, and conscious that I had only brought with me a limited amount of sustenance, Ralph instructed me to raid the station buffet for as many pasties as I could, as well as getting our tea cans filled. I was to be very glad of his advice later.

We set off again, gingerly down the steep drop to St. David's all under clear signals. As we were going to rescue a stranded train we were travelling under what was known as 'A' headlights, meaning we were classified as a priority working. Even so it must seemed strange that to the travelling public, we in appearance a mere goods train, empty at that, and having preference over any passenger working at St David's.

After Cowley Bridge we ran as far as Coleford Junction before we were routed 'wrong road', cautiously arriving at the stranded train which had stopped in the cutting.

It was now the turn of others, but first I pulled the fire back under door, and with the fire-doors open we both settled back in our electrically lit, coal heated cab to wait events.

The night dragged on and we both dozed off from time to time. Our original tea cans had also long been emptied and I recall at one stage melting snow in the tea can and boiling this inside the firebox to make a fresh brew. We were relieved around dawn by a crew from Okehampton who had themselves arrived on a light engine, also running wrong-road. We took this engine back to Okehampton and returned to Exeter courtesy of a BR minibus. Curiously the roads in places were clearer than the railway which was still blocked in several places.

After the snow came the floods. I was booked on at 5.25 am for the 6.25 am departure from Exmouth Junction goods yard with a freight for Yeoford. I was with driver Les Wellings and our engine was a 'Blackmotor'. It was, and had been raining stair-rods for some time, but at this stage we went away as normal and eventually arrived, without incident at Yeoford, except for the fact there was water everywhere around. I learned later that we the last train to pass over the Downes Bridge at Crediton, before it was shut due to water damage to the piers.

We proceeded to shunt the yard at Yeoford as usual, at the time both of us questioning who in their right mind would even bother to come and collect any goods delivered to the station in these conditions. All the while the water level was rising around us, so much so that the poor shunter: we all called him 'Elvis' - although what his real name was we never knew, was forced to balance on top of a ground signal just to keep his feet dry. Despite his tenacity at insisting on wading through the flood water when necessary, we all had to agree that eventually it was becoming too deep to continue and for safety sake we put the engine in the up bay platform and threw out the fire. Understandably the contact of hot coals and ash with sodden ground resulted in clouds of steam erupting all around. With the engine stabled: perhaps a more accurate term might be moored, we were rescued by rowing boat (honestly) and taken across to another watery location, this time the 'Mare and Foal' public house where we had time for a pint before being rescued (again) by BR mini-bus. We had to agree, the lot of the loco crew was very trying, having to seemingly end our shift out of necessity in a pub.

I have mentioned earlier my first week on the Exeter - Salisbury main line, the first day of this being especially busy. I was booked with Driver Frank Watts, a real gentleman and one of several men with the same surname at Exmouth Junction. We were booked 'Up 10.30 am Waterloo, engine prepared', and had an unrebuilt 'West Country' No. 34015 'Exmouth'. I recall the load was either 10 or 11 coaches, whilst to add to the concentration, we had a passenger on the footplate, a local bank-manager and which in turn meant he had to be accompanied by a loco inspector, in this case Edgar Snow. I had no problem with the Inspector: indeed it was he who had initiated me into the art of firing.

We set off from 'Central, the footplate perhaps seeming slightly cramped with the extra individuals on board. It was a different matter if you were running light, extra bods made scant difference when an engine required little firing, but on a main line service it was a totally different matter. So it was bend the back and off we go, and we reached our booked stop at Yeovil Junction on time. Now though the fun was about to start, for as Frank braked to a stop, so the water in the boiler surged forward and in the progress jammed one of the injector clack valves in the open position: these were supposedly one way valves allowing cold water into the boiler from the injectors but not allowing water or steam to flow from the boiler back the other way. Now though water was pouring back through the injector overflow pipe under the cab and which on meeting the air was instantly ejected as steam, it was like having a blowing safety valve under the cab. Three of us, the driver, inspector and myself knew instantly what was happening, uppermost in our minds was the risk of losing so much water from the boiler there was a risk of uncovering a plug. With the knowledge then that if we did manage to save the situation the water would already be seriously depleted, I climbed on to the rear of the tender to top up the tank with as much water as possible, while Frank was wrestling with

Evening light with a 'Woolworth' between Exeter Central and Exeter St. David's. Admiring the sight, fellow enthusiast Richard Beavan is enjoying his fish and chips - with much vinegar!

Above - Bulleids, original and after' rebuilding, 34015 'Exmouth' seen earlier and 34095 'Brentor'. The depot breakdown train, with its red liveried coaching stock, is stabled on the right.

Opposite page - No. 34030 'Watersmeet', this time with all wheels where they should be!

David Smith

the controls on the footplate. The Inspector meanwhile had jumped off the footplate and grabbed a conveniently placed ladder, normally used for affixing the roof boards onto carriages. He placed the ladder against the engine casing and by climbing up was able to slide open the hatch which afforded access to the actual valve. The remedy was now in the time honoured railway tradition, several hefty blows with the coal pick! Luckily this worked, had it not, the engine would have been a failure. By comparison, the rest of the trip and likewise our return were uneventful. I think our bank manager friend even enjoyed it, something about where do you find a bank-manager: not in a cupboard, but enveloped in steam on a footplate. (This was a disadvantage with the original Bulleid type, the clack valves could only be reached with a ladder, there being no running boards to stand upon.)

On the opposite page, the illustration shows No. 34095 'Brentor', alongside a set of red flags and lamps, a reminder of one of the less salubrious events of my railway career at Exmouth Junction. This was a run-away into the turntable pit, and for which I was totally responsible. It happened in 1964, just after we had been 'adopted' by the Western Region and on an occasion when I was booked 'Midnight to 8.00 am' - 'Turning'. Contrary to what might have appeared the obvious from the duty description, this did not involve much actual turning of engines, but instead the seemingly straightforward task of moving them into their correct positions ready for the next duty etc. I was of course booked to a driver, and whilst in theory we were supposed to always work together, in practice it made life a lot easier if we worked separately on occasions, it was also then less of a rush. Anyway, I was trying to be helpful and went to move No. 34030 'Watersmeet' into a clearance position: meaning out of the way to allow another engine to be moved. No. 34030 was standing where No. 34095 is seen. Unfortunately, although the engine moved forward alright, it would not stop as efficiently as usual, because the steam pressure was too low to operate the brake effectively, we thus ran away stopping with the front bogie wheels in the turntable pit. The turntable was not in use at the time and the obvious thing to have done would have been set it to face the arriving engine - I always did after that! Likewise I should have checked the steam pressure from the gauge before starting - I did that afterwards as well.

But to return to that night. Having firstly satisfied myself I did not need an immediate change of under garments, I dashed back inside the shed to inform the running foreman, Jack Tiley, of my indiscretion - No. 34030 that is. His reaction was understandable and totally unprintable here. I learnt later this was partly because someone else had done exactly the same thing with a 'Merchant Navy' a week previous. Hence the lamps and flags seen in the photograph protecting the turntable line whilst repairs were effected. All in all, not one of my better moments. (Apropos nothing at all, I once owned a nameplate from No. 34030 'Watersmeet'.)

This type of incident also warrants perhaps a little more in the telling, for when our turntable was out of action - for whatever reason that is, we had to take recourse to the turning facility at the Western Region shed at St David's. Consequently for about a week at a time there might be as many as six Southern engines coupled together making their way to and fro. Neither was it a popular job, there could well be a queue there already and the WR men always took priority at their own shed. In addition, apart

from the obvious problem of balancing a 'Merchant Navy' on the Western's 'Hornby-Dublo' turntable, it was hand operated and we had then to push it round. This was hard going, we were used to our vacuum driven equipment, anything else was unnecessary work, although in my case probably a just dessert.

Another amusing tale, again relating to turntables, concerns the workings to Ilfracombe, and involving the original Bulleid pacifics. I had occasion to be on one of these for the first time with, I think, No. 34081 '92 Squadron'. No one had forewarned me of anything, so having worked down, uneventfully I would add, we took the engine for servicing and turning at the small shed.

Now the turntable at Ilfracombe was sited so that half was in a semi-circle cutting in the rock face, and when the wind was blowing, as it often did - and you'd got a slab sided engine…...you can see where this is going…...it could be somewhat difficult to persuade the turntable to stop. This is exactly what happened, no not round and round as in the films, but we did go around completely twice that is until the wind stopped and I managed to engage the locking pin with the engine now (luckily) facing the correct direction for the return working. Others experienced similar difficulties, the situation made more difficult when they managed to stop but with the engine still facing the way they had started from. (The cut away in the rock face can still be seen in the large, very private, car park of a local electronics company.)

Left - *1 August 1962. No. 34074 '46 Squadron' makes a spirited departure from Ilfracombe and passes the locomotive shed and its infamous turntable! The train is the 4.50 pm stopping service to Exeter Central and Exmouth . (The locomotive would likely be changed at Exeter Central.)*
Tony Molyneaux

Right - *No. 34076 '41 Squadron' arriving at Exeter St David's from direction of Cowley bridge and prior to proceeding to 'Central. Exeter St. David's was one the stations in the country where it was possible to depart for London in either direction - dependent upon whether the preference was for the Southern or Western routes. When the SR line to Plymouth via Okehampton existed, the same applied for Plymouth passengers.*

THE INTERLOPER AT ST. DAVID'S

Above and opposite top - *This time it is No. 34066 'Spitfire' that is arriving - No. 4694 the 'Pannier Tank' also visible, awaiting banking duty. No. 34066 displays a headcode indication this was working from Padstow. The single disc displayed at the centre of the buffer beam was the code for banking engines between the WR and SR Exeter stations. The lean-to structure behind the Pannier-Tank is part of the Exeter St. David's goods depot and still stands in the 21st century although in derelict condition.*

Opposite bottom - *'W' No 31914, with the worst over - well for this trip at least. The engine has arrived at Exeter Central having pushed an eastbound freight up the bank. It is believed the weight limit for these engines was slightly less than for the 'Z' class.*
Peter Elliott

Left - Passing Exeter Middle Signal box, is 'N' No. 31840 with a train for Ilfracombe.
Above - From the footplate of the banking engine No. 4694 seem earlier (- the shovel on the side of the bunker is the cause of the curved shape), another member of the 'N' class, No. 31845 arrives at St. David's where it will pause for the banking engine to attach ready for the climb to 'Central. On the right hand side is the former Cadbury's depot.

Summer at St. David's. AWS fitted 'N' class, No. 31855 arrives with ballast from Meldon. Most of our 'N' class engines were in dirty brown livery, indeed I recall only ever cleaning one and that was soon after I started in 1959. It was not that they were not supposed to be cleaned, simply that they were always on the go and never on shed long enough to receive our attention. Speaking of cleaning, I recall one day when several of us had started work on a filthy Bulleid, No. 34058 'Sir Frederick Pile'. We were making a good job as well, one side was already covered in swirls of paraffin and oil prior to this being wiped off. We were about to commence the other side when the engine was commandeered at short notice for a London train - I recall to replace a failed locomotive. Anyway off in went, filthy on one side and sparkling on the other. Unfortunately it was seen and noted in this condition. The depot subsequently received a 'Please Report' note from Headquarters as to why this had taken place.

Not quite black liveried: there is just a trace of green around the cab number. Underneath the grime is No. 34086 '219 Squadron' setting off from St. David's with a train for Okehampton and Plymouth.

Arriving at Exeter St David's Platform 3 from Okehampton, is 'N' class 2-6-0 No. 31845 with a light load of just two coaches.
Peter Elliott

A JOB FOR LIFE?

The rundown of steam at 'The Junction' had started even before I had joined. In 1959 when I started on the railway, the BR Modernisation plan was already four years old. As a youth before that time, I could not comment with any experience on what had gone before, although later I recall some of the older drivers bemoaning the things that were passing. Looking back I now know that is a facet of human life, as a youngster we accept change, as we ourselves get older we hanker back to 'the good old days'.

Even so I was present to see, if not work, on the last of the 'T9s', although as mentioned earlier I also missed working on the 'E1R' tanks. It was hard to imagine the former 4-4-0s, little by modern standards working express trains 40 years earlier. But the men I now regarded as senior drivers were the ones who had started as cleaners and firemen in the days of the old London & South Western Railway, cleaners at the old Exmouth Junction shed and who had seen engines getting bigger and more modern as time passed. The reaction of some even in wartime, when the 'Bulleid' pacifics had arrived was one of pride. 'Now we have got something really special to show those Western men'.

But for the present at least it was again our neighbours, the Western men who once more had the latest most modern designs, with their 'Warship' class diesels. I had first been aware of these in the final months of my train spotting days at St. David's, green boxes that made a lot of noise as they departed and with the crew seemingly sitting doing nothing in the cab. I would find out later that in those early days there was often much doubt if they would ever start again every time they stopped!

We had had our diesels as well, years before I had started, the SR's own main line diesels (10201-3) had for a while worked services to and from Waterloo. These were supplemented by two similar machines originating on the LMS. No one said much about those times, probably because the period in question had in effect been somewhat brief. Once again then steam reigned supreme.

But if we had but known, there was massive change going on behind the scenes. For over ten years British Railways had in reality altered little since nationalisation, the regions and their respective boundaries had remained almost the same, and whilst new steam engines in the form of the 'Standard' types had arrived to consign the older designs to oblivion, elsewhere everyone carried on exactly as before - save perhaps for a change to the insignia on the uniforms and headings to the paperwork. The Southern Railway was alive and well: or so we thought.

It came then as a shock when the rumours started to fly about concerning a transfer to the Western Region. Even more when this was quickly followed by stories that a number of branch lines, including many west of Exeter were under threat. Some regarded this as little more than scaremongering. In any organisation there will always be the rumour mongers, although they added weight to their argument with comments such as 'well look how difficult it is to get staff' and the like.

Still though it seemed inconceivable that change in the form it eventually took was even thinkable. We took solace that although we might transfer to the Western and perhaps have to learn a few of their engines - even their routes, ours was the better laid out shed and we had the more modern steam engines anyway. Logic dictated if there were to be casualties, it would be 'down the road' not with us.

'800' No. 80036 at Honiton in 1964. We had arrived on the 12.35 pm up stopping service from Exeter and were waiting our path to return with a similar working to Exeter Central later in the day.

The romance has gone, in the rain it could be a dirty and cold job. Taken in the last years of the shed - note the DMU stabled in the background. The engine is No. 34063 '229 Squadron' which remained at Exmouth Junction until May 1963. From here it moved for a few months to Brighton and then finally to Salisbury where it was withdrawn in 1965.

The formal announcement, when it came, of a transfer to the WR, not just for us but all our lines as well, came as a shock. But we continued as before, initially there was no change. Save that is for the odd WR engine that appeared at Exmouth Junction - we put that down to being suitable replacements for some of our own older engines, whilst at some of the stations, particularly west of Exeter, chocolate and cream signage replaced some of the older green Southern items. Personally I was still loving my life on the footplate, perhaps it was even with a sneaking wish that I might in the future now have even more opportunity with different steam engines, some of the larger WR types I had 'spotted' at St. David's, a 'Castle perhaps?

With the WR take over of our former lines so did their own plans to replace steam as quickly as possible on our principal services. Up to that time I had no experience on diesels of any type, my confidence not exactly encouraged one day when waiting with a steam engine at Meldon on one occasion, when my driver and I observed a passenger train arriving from the direction of Plymouth with flames and smoke billowing from the roof of the approaching 'Warship' diesel. Even to our untrained eyes this could not be right and we were quick in attempting to attract the attention of the crew to what we honestly believed was something they were unaware of but looked extremely serious. By means of sign language, they indicated everything was perfectly normal, it certainly seemed far from normal to us, but they passed us in the direction of Okehampton and when we subsequently left for Exeter some time later, there was no sign of any roasted engine en-route. (I learned later this was one of the trials of the early steam-heating boilers fitted to these engines which displayed a propensity to erupt at times. Shades then of the occasional volcanic effects from the original Mr. Bulleid design, but now one which was recommended not to be extinguished from the nearest water column'.)

Gradually though steam began to drift away and was replaced by various WR diesel types. The drivers went on courses, most welcoming the change and eager to learn, to do so meant they kept their job and which in the future would also be an all together easier and far less physically demanding task. For us firemen however it was a worrying time, would there be a job for us at all? It seemed that in total fewer drivers were in fact needed whilst again the rumour machine pointed to the fact that the diesel multiple units we saw wandering around on the various branches were single manned.

Some of the more concerned firemen, especially the senior men and those with families, were the first to go, although this was at the time voluntary. Their logic being that if redundancy was coming they would rather have the pick of the jobs outside instead of having to take what was left at the end.

Charlie Smaile the new Shedmaster, Horace Moore had retired by this time, could offer no solace either. At least for me and the others who stayed, it meant even more main line work even if the engines were in poor mechanical as well external condition.

It was ASLEF, our union, who saved the day for most firemen. At the time BR had a policy where they wished to introduce single-manning on all diesel hauled trains. This they stated was perfectly safe as there was a 'dead mans' handle - or pedal, in each engine, and which, unless pressure continued to be exerted, would automatically apply the brakes. (A somewhat more sophisticated system is in operation today.) But there was the counter argument that the train heating boiler fitted to the new diesel engines required regular attention. This was perfectly true. Like the early diesels, these boilers, necessary because at the time most coaching stock was still steam heated, were far from reliable, as witness our observations at Meldon. They and their associated controls were also located behind the driving cabs and so it would not have been possible for a driver to both drive and attend to the boiler. The potential for cold passengers won the day and we firemen were thus sent away to various places to receive training on these oil fired boilers as fitted to the D63xx, D70xx, D8xx, and D10xx types, which were all four of the main line diesel engines operated by the WR. I recall the boiler types as being of 'Clayton', 'Spanner', and 'Stone-Vapor' manufacture.

Overnight then it seemed as if the cloud of redundancy disappeared and with so many men from my grade having left, I was now one of an almost endangered species and found myself regularly rostered as 'secondman' on trains not only over the former SR lines but also the WR routes to Plymouth, Bristol and Taunton. Even so it was not all fun, especially when attempting to start up the 'Spanner Mk.1' train-heat boiler on a D8xx 'Warship'. Under such circumstances the procedure was not exactly as per the textbook. Instead, we would,, "...press the relevant buttons and retire outside the boiler compartment", closing the door firmly behind us. One of my colleagues put it slightly differently, "Light the blue touch paper and run like………". We would then wait for "ignition" but hopefully not "lift-off" as the fumes ignited hopefully before too much oil had flowed. Should ignition not take place within the anticipated time period, the oil would still have continued to flow. Now there was the need to turn off the supply, but to open the door would result in an inrush of air which might in itself be sufficient to create ignition. More than one second man was the victim of singed eyebrows and the like. We may smile

Post 1964 at Exmouth Junction. Steam has gone - well almost. Engines that were in good order had been retained by the Southern Region and transferred to their own remaining steam depots, mainly Salisbury, Weymouth, Eastleigh or Nine Elms. Those that were left and which were in effect now Western Region stock were in poor order and did not last long. The few remaining steam turns were also now handled from either Salisbury or Yeovil, servicing facilities only being provided here for steam until 1965. At this stage a few diesels were allocated, but they did not need a turntable and so this was disposed of in late 1966: the depot closed completely in 1967. It remained derelict, an eyesore where once there had been hustle and bustle, a victim of change that could not have been foreseen even a decade earlier. At that time it would have been reasonable to assume new forms of traction would still need servicing facilities - indeed Exmouth Junction was far better laid out than the cramped facilities at the steam shed at St. David's. Notice then the covered accommodation: St. David's lost its roof but was retained as a stabling point for some years, engines being maintained in the open. With the removal of the machines, so too did the men leave, some - a few, transferred to the new traction, although for most it was either redundancy or a change to a totally different type of role.

nowadays but the potential was in fact rather more serious.

The drivers too, after a life time on steam and brought up to the maxim, "...to carry on at all costs…" were now also faced with a dilemma. The new traction had numerous 'fault lights' to worry about which some of the older men admitted they found confusing. Now also rather than being with a regular driver, I found myself with various different men. Some of the senior WR drivers had also learnt the road from Exeter to Salisbury and from Exeter to Ilfracombe and so began working trains over these routes. I learnt a lot from these men, often having little else to do in the cab, I could watch their different techniques for driving - and more importantly stopping. It was all good experience, whilst when something did go wrong they would sometimes genuinely ask our opinion as to how to resolve a situation, perhaps thinking that us youngsters might somehow have a better grasp of the "technicals".

One specific example of a failure was with driver Fred Clark, very much a senior man. We were on an up passenger train from Barnstaple with a D63xx. Everything was fine as we left Barnstaple but we only got as far as the first station out at Chapelton, when the engine failed. As we were within station limits my driver instructed me to find a phone and call for assistance. The station was locked up, unfortunately too, so was the signal box, it being switched out at that time. I reported back and was promptly told to "break in". I duly did, via a judicious tap to a pane of glass in the door. Through this I was able to release the window catch and climb in. Now for the easy bit, a quick call to the man at Barnstaple Junction, but not before he had recovered himself, hardly expecting his telephone line from a supposedly closed signal box to suddenly burst into life. Having recovered his equilibrium he soon arranged for a locomotive from his station to arrive and pull us back to where we had started from. Somehow a fitter was also summoned, goodness knows from where, as there were certainly no diesel fitters at Barnstaple. With a few tweaks and the like from this man we were on our way again.

On another occasion I was back on steam: we did get swapped about as well, and working a loaded ballast train from Meldon. Our engine was a rebuilt, 'Battle of Britain', hardly ideal motive power for this type of heavy train, but by now it was sometimes a case of whatever engine there was available, all the 'S15' types having been withdrawn. We should have had a clear run, certainly as far as Coleford Junction, but were instead stopped at North Tawton. Here we were informed that the train ahead of us, the 'Up Brighton', and 'Warship' hauled had failed in the section between North Tawton and Bow. 'Control' at Exeter had instructed that we shunt our own train into a siding and then run 'wrong road' to Bow,

and from here reverse to assist the stranded train from the front. We were to continue assisting as far as Exeter St. David's.

Absolutely no problem, although naturally the service was somewhat late arriving at Exeter. Here though the reception was nothing short of tumultuous, you'd have thought it was royalty arriving, such was the reception of the spotters on the platform overjoyed at seeing steam triumph over the diesel. The euphoria was to be short lived as a fitter was already waiting and within minutes the 'Warship' had burst into life again. We simply hooked off and ran to Exmouth Junction to finish our turn of duty.

I mentioned earlier my new found knowledge of diesel traction meant I was at times also booked to work on the Western main line. This was the case on one occasion when booked with a St. David's man on a fitted freight to Bristol, again with a 'Warship'. (I should add that the train heating boiler would certainly not be needed on a freight, but the working agreement reached between ASLEF and BR meant locomotive hauled diesel trains would continue to be double manned.) This driver was also not averse to letting me drive and consequently I had the 'handle'. I also thought I was doing quite well, until that is he leaned across and reminded me in genuinely polite terms that I was actually driving a freight and not the 'Cornish Riviera'. I took the point and slowed down, gently coming down the gradient from Whiteball Tunnel to be greeted by a red colour light signal at the bottom. Being second-man it was my job to dismount and use the telephone to the signal box at Taunton, but as I was about to remount the engine, I noticed a large pool of oil under the front bogie. I pointed this out to the driver who identified it as hydraulic oil from the transmission. We advised the signalman and when the clear aspect indicated, proceeded gently to Taunton where the engine was failed. The train meanwhile was placed in a siding and we returned home 'pass'.

On another occasion, again on the Western main line, I was secondman in a somewhat crowded cab as in addition to the driver we had with us a number of other men 'learning the road' (- or it may even have been 'learning the traction' - whatever -). This time it was with one of the bigger D10xx types fitted with two separate engines of 1,350 hp each. The load was also heavy as it was a main line passenger train. We left Taunton heading for Exeter in normal order, but within a few moments one engine shut down completely. With the climb to Whiteball approaching, my driver asked me, "Can you drive this thing?", I responded that I could and he thus left me to it whilst he and the others went back to try and effect some sort of remedy on the dead engine. I had to stand up in the cab to watch the sleepers slowly passing underneath and so check we were in fact

No longer would the impressive 'Merchant navy' class engines be seen running between Exeter and Exmouth Junction. No 35018 'British India Line' returning to the depot after working the down, 11.00 am 'Atlantic Coast Express' from Waterloo in 1963.

still moving forwards. Fortunately the combined brains of those travelling worked their magic and the second engine was started to power us down the other side and a slightly late arrival at St. David's. It also went to prove the advantage of having two separate power units in one locomotive.

Despite being an avowed steam man, I have to admit one of best memories of those diesel days was on a 'Warship' - one I would add that was working well, on a Salisbury train with a Southern driver. It was also one of the faster workings. Approaching Salisbury we were brought to a stand at the outer home signal. Expecting perhaps to be here for a few minutes, my driver went back to use the 'on-board facilities'. The signal though cleared with a few moments leaving me with the obvious dilemma, do I move the train or await my driver's return? Having been schooled as a Southern man, I had been brought up to the premise of not losing time, it was but a moment to jump into the driver's seat, let off the brakes and with a quick 'toot' on the horn I powered up and started the train away. At this point my driver returned and I, fully expecting a right rollicking, immediately got up to relinquish the seat but keeping my foot on the 'deadmans' pedal. He though, moved past me and sat in my seat with the words, "You take her in son". I could not have been more proud. It may have been a diesel, but here I was taking this important express into Salisbury without a further word from him. Stopping in the right place was I knew the most difficult, but we managed fine. As we stopped we were relieved by a London crew, the driver of which on seeing me commented, "Blimey, they're getting younger all the time". I wish I could remember that Southern man's name, just to thank him for one of the high spots in my career.

But after the highs came the lows as I witnessed not just the run down of Exmouth Junction but the singling of the Southern main line, at the time even considered to be a prelude to complete closure. Luckily someone saw sense on that one. Unfortunately there was no similar reprieve for the lines west of Exeter and the short stub that survives today as far as Barnstaple is but nothing compared with what I had been fortunate to experience.

Mr Moore though had been wrong, it was not a job for life, barely for a decade instead. Would I have changed it - never. Do I still miss it - hardly a day goes by when I do not think of something from those days.

No. 35013 'Blue Funnel' under the hopper at Exmouth Junction.

Mark Abbott

'BLUE PETER'

On 14 August 1966, we learned that a special was coming down the Southern line from Waterloo behind LNER 'A2' No. 60532 'Blue Peter'. Being interested in all things steam and never having seen one of this class previously, I ventured up to the top of Honiton bank to watch it perform as it reached the top of the climb on the down run. Unfortunately it never made it, having to stop for a 'blow-up' on the London side of the tunnel.

No doubt with judicious use of the pricker and several choice adjectives, sufficient steam pressure was eventually restored and the train continued to Exeter where the 'A2' ran back to Exmouth Junction for servicing. I was booked late turn 'spare' on the day and with nothing waiting for me, asked the Foreman if I might go and 'muck-in' on the engine. I was told to help myself so went over and ended up putting the bag of the water column in the tender. Whilst it was filling I happened to glance forward along the top of the boiler to see a small wisp of steam emanating from somewhere on top of the firebox in front of the cab.

With the watering complete, and I have to admit being a bit nosey, I walked across the top of the coal, thence over the cab roof and discovered that the whistle top: which on LNER locomotives had the 'bell' cast integrally with the spindle, had broken clean off, the top lying on the handrail of the fireman's side. I went to pick it up and ended up doing a juggling act - it was hot, but somehow managed to drop it into my jacket pocket. With that I dismounted and went off to show the Foreman.

He was certainly not best pleased. An engine without 'an audible means of approach' is a technical failure. A fitter was thus dispatched to try and first of all find an SR, BR or WR whistle and then also fit it. For whatever reason this could not be done, neither did anyone find it possible to shut off the steam supply to the whistle, the latter especially seeming rather strange, but then fitters always know best.

Following much discussion, the result of which being that they would probably be happier to see the back of it, 'Blue Peter' went on its way without a whistle and for that day at least a continuous slight escape of steam. I was allowed to keep the top I had found, which I had for some years, although like my nameplate collection, all have since found other homes.

Strangers in the camp. **Top** - *'A4' No. 60024 'Kingfisher' on the final stretches of the climb to Exeter Central: D7048 was acting as the banker. The train was a special Waterloo - Exeter St. David's and return working on 27 March 1966.* **Bottom** - *No. 60532 'Blue Peter' stalled due to shortage and steam (poor coal) on Honiton bank at the head of 9 coaches on another special, 14 August 1966.*   S J Healey

MEMORIES

Top left - Exeter bound*, No. 35024 'East Asiatic Company' passing Axminster in 1964. Our train was on the right, another stopping service, which will follow when the main line service has passed. I recall one occasion with Driver Alfie Spragg on No. 80036 when we were passing the Sidmouth Junction outer home signal at Fenny Bridges. We just had two coaches behind but suddenly the brakes came on hard. As we were within station limits, the guard quickly went to carry out train protection It transpired a small rubber disc in the brake handle had developed a hole. We were eventually piloted back to Exeter with an 'Ivatt Class 2'. Class '6' motive power then for a 2-coach train!* **Top right** *- Another 'Merchant Navy', this one No. 35026 'Lamport & Holt Line' travelling east leaving Blackboy Tunnel near Exmouth Junction on a west country railtour, 15 October 1966.* **Right** *- Another idle moment: taken from the footplate of a BR 'Class 4' tank, as another 'Standard', No 75022, passes us on the main line at Seaton Junction, heading for Salisbury, in 1964.*

No. 34063 '229 Squadron' arriving at Exeter St. David's on Friday 28 August 1959 with the up 'Atlantic Coast Express'. Assuming the train was running to time, it would now be shortly after 12.00 pm, this being one of two portions of the train to arrive here, one from Padstow: due at Exeter Central at 12.12 pm, and another portion from Torrington: due at Exeter Central at 12.24 pm. Six minutes were then allowed at Exeter Central for both portions to be combined, plus an engine change to a 'Merchant Navy' ready for a 12.30 pm departure to Waterloo calling only at Salisbury. At other times of the year and on different days of the week, there were slight variations in both the timing and stopping places.   *Tony Molyneaux*

Also on 28 August 1959, No. 34110 '66 Squadron' leaves Exeter St. David's with what was reported as an all stations stopping service from Exeter Central to Plymouth via Okehampton.

Tony Molyneaux

'T9' No 30729, which spent a year allocated to Exmouth Junction from April 1960, seen here on pilot duty at Exeter Central on Saturday 16 July 1960. The engine may well have arrived or be due for another train, but had been 'borrowed' to shunt the coaches seen. This was a common practice at busy periods, the normal Exeter Central station pilot for years being an 'M7' tank, subsequently replaced by an 'Ivatt'. The number of passengers with suitcases are a give-away to the fact it is the summer season. There are also a number modern and older era comparisons, the locomotive for example dating from 1899 whilst on the opposite platform is modern BR Mk1 stock and beyond the railway boundary contemporary concrete building construction and a tower crane.

Tony Molyneaux

Leaving Ilfracombe at the start of the steep climb from the station. 'N' class (Woolworth) No. 31841 on the 1.30 pm stopping passenger service to Barnstaple Junction, 1 August 1962.

Tony Molyneaux

A few minutes later, at 1.48 pm, No. 34033 'Chard' arrives from the opposite direction with the 8.10 am stopping service from Salisbury. 143 miles in three and half hours, but that did include something like 35 intermediate stops.

Tony Molyneaux

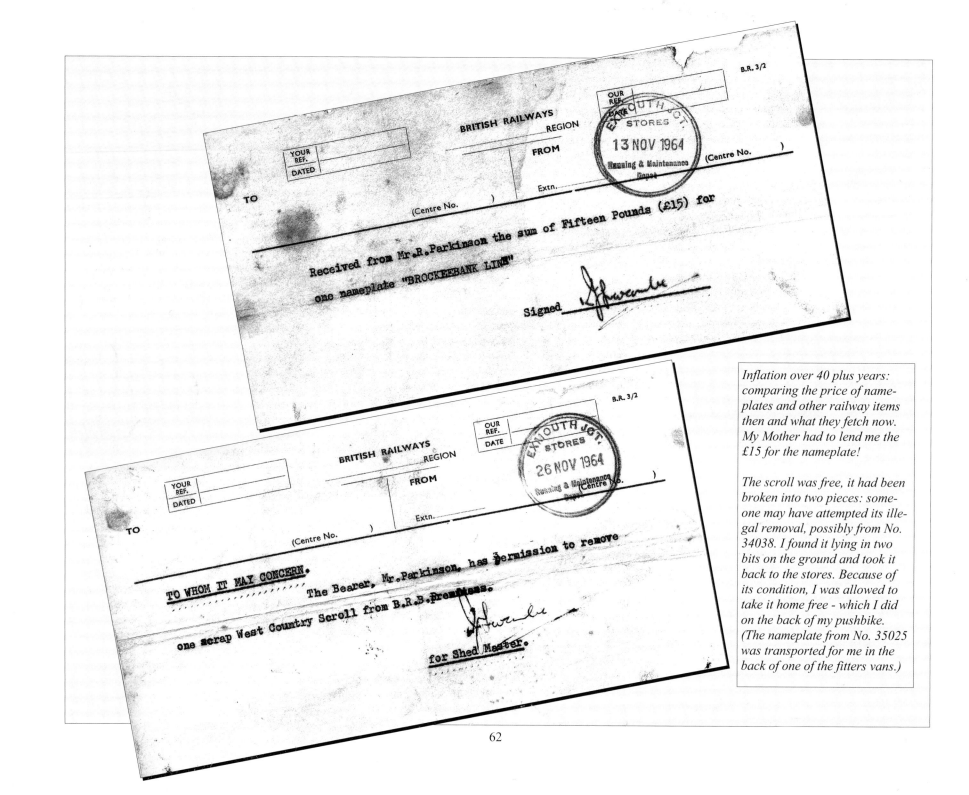

Inflation over 40 plus years: comparing the price of nameplates and other railway items then and what they fetch now. My Mother had to lend me the £15 for the nameplate!

The scroll was free, it had been broken into two pieces: someone may have attempted its illegal removal, possibly from No. 34038. I found it lying in two bits on the ground and took it back to the stores. Because of its condition, I was allowed to take it home free - which I did on the back of my pushbike. (The nameplate from No. 35025 was transported for me in the back of one of the fitters vans.)

A few minutes later, at 1.48 pm, No. 34033 'Chard' arrives from the opposite direction with the 8.10 am stopping service from Salisbury. 143 miles in three and half hours, but that did include something like 35 intermediate stops.

Tony Molyneaux

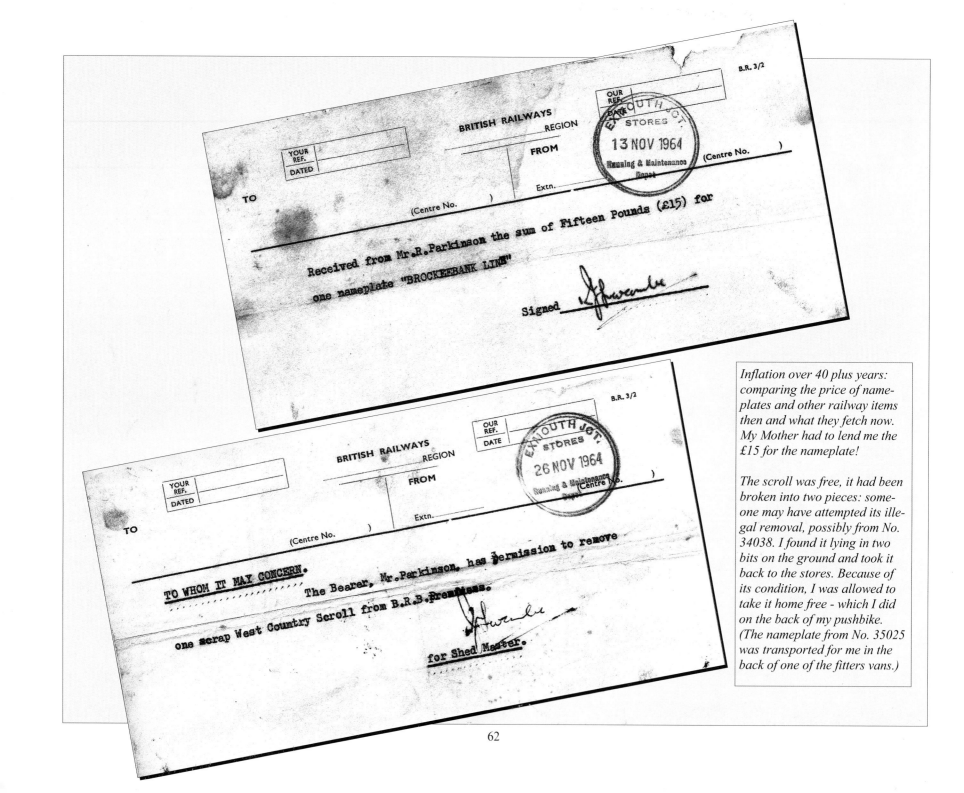

Inflation over 40 plus years: comparing the price of nameplates and other railway items then and what they fetch now. My Mother had to lend me the £15 for the nameplate!

The scroll was free, it had been broken into two pieces: someone may have attempted its illegal removal, possibly from No. 34038. I found it lying in two bits on the ground and took it back to the stores. Because of its condition, I was allowed to take it home free - which I did on the back of my pushbike. (The nameplate from No. 35025 was transported for me in the back of one of the fitters vans.)

The view from Platform 4 at Exeter St. David's on 26 August 1959. In Platform 5 is a Paddington bound WR 'Warship' class No. D809 'Champion' with 41xx No. 4176 in Platform 4. It was views like this that I witnessed as a youthful spotter and a member of the 'Platform 5 Group', which encouraged what was to be my early working life on the railway. Had I but known at the time, I would have noticed the Southern 'Z' class engine in the banking siding in the distance. 26 August 1959.
Tony Molyneaux

Memories at Exeter Central. 'N' class 2-6-0 No. 31845 shunting stock after which it will then run light to Exmouth Junction. Meanwhile No. 35023 'Holland-Afrika Line' awaits setting back on to the second portion of the train before final departure for the main line to Salisbury and Waterloo. *Peter Elliott*